The Chamber of
HOLY OF HOLIES

The Chamber of
HOLY OF HOLIES

*Granted access to supernatural
encounters through my prayer closet*

Prophet Kofi O. Yeboah

XULON PRESS

Xulon Press
2301 Lucien Way #415
Maitland, FL 32751
407.339.4217
www.xulonpress.com

© 2021 by Prophet Kofi O. Yeboah

All rights reserved solely by the author. The author guarantees all contents are original and do not infringe upon the legal rights of any other person or work. No part of this book may be reproduced in any form without the permission of the author.

Due to the changing nature of the Internet, if there are any web addresses, links, or URLs included in this manuscript, these may have been altered and may no longer be accessible. The views and opinions shared in this book belong solely to the author and do not necessarily reflect those of the publisher. The publisher therefore disclaims responsibility for the views or opinions expressed within the work.

Unless otherwise indicated, Scripture quotations taken from the New King James Version (NKJV). Copyright © 1982 by Thomas Nelson, Inc. Used by permission. All rights reserved.

Scripture quotations taken from the Holy Bible, New Living Translation (NLT). Copyright ©1996, 2004, 2007 by Tyndale House Foundation. Used by permission of Tyndale House Publishers, Inc.

Printed in the United States of America

Paperback ISBN-13: 978-1-66281-959-9
Ebook ISBN-13: 978-1-66281-960-5

Table of Contents:

Foreword vii
Acknowledgements ix
Introduction. xi

Chapter I 1
   Power of Prayer 3
   Purpose of Prayer 5
   The Value of Prayer 13
   The Golden Censer 15

Chapter II. 21
   The Presence of God 23
   Dwelling in the Presence 33

Chapter III. 37
   Child of God 39
   True Identity 43
   Royal Priesthood 47

Chapter IV 53
   Seek and You Shall Find 55
   Deep Longing 59

Chapter V 65
   Deep Is Calling unto Deep 67

Chapter VI 73
   I Know Him, Not I Know About Him 75
   Religion Kills. 77

Chapter VII 85
   How Do I Do It?. 87

About the Author 91

Foreword

When l was called upon to write a foreword to this book, I did not hesitate at all. When I first met Kofi Yeboah, I saw a person who enjoys the presence of God in worship, prayer, and in-depth study of the Word of God. I have had the privilege to witness his ministerial capacity and grace. Kofi Yeboah has written an unnervingly simple yet deeply profound book that goes beyond your normal how-to be in the presence of God and maintain deep consistency in fellowship with God. I am confident this book will be a tremendous blessing to empower the reader in the development of their prayer life and communion with God.

Kofi Yeboah goes beyond addressing the regular pitfalls in divine communion with God and gets into the deeper issues of the core-values and fundamentals of one's relationship with God.

The author draws upon a wealth of insight through his wide exposure to great men and women of God, authors, and many Christ followers. The reader will be challenged to read more about the passionate presentation from this book. I commend it to every leader and Christian.

Dr. Lawrence Tetteh
World Miracle Outreach

Acknowledgements:

I would like to thank God for the grace and resilience over the years to complete this book. Through the hard times, research, and prayer, He gave me more insight to communicate it through this book, and I am truly thankful. I want to show my sincere gratitude to my spiritual father and mentor, Rev. Samuel Awuku-Gyekye, Senior Pastor of International Central Gospel Church (ICGC, Royal Temple, Accra, Ghana), for his unstoppable counsel, impact, unwavering support, and prayer, which has made me the person I am today. His commitment to personal prayer and his attitude to being in God's presence shaped my life and gave me one of the secrets to effective service in the kingdom of God. I salute you, sir! My sincere thanks and appreciation go to Dr. Frank Opoku Amoako, Senior Pastor of Destiny Life Chapel International, for his immense expertise in authorship, his counsel in arrangement, his total support, and encouragement toward this book. I would like to also thank my good friend Rev. Cephas Kafui Agbesi, Senior Pastor of Honeywell Worship Center (New York), for his support in editorial work and prayer. My sincere thank you goes to my friend Mr. Sefakor Adzanku (Communication Specialist, MA in

Experimental Psychology, Central Washington University, USA), for his tireless editorial work on the third draft of this work: God bless you! To my covenant brother, the revelator, Pastor Benjamin Opoku, Senior Pastor of Salvation Nest Chapel (New York), God bless you for being there through this process in our midnight prayers, encouragement, refinement, and your belief in this project.

To my wonderful wife, Henrietta, my encourager and backbone, thank you for all the love, supports, reminders, prayers, and encouragement you gave me and keep giving me during the writing of this book. To my children, Janai, Neriah, and Raphael, you gave me a lot of inspiration to complete this book.

My sincere thanks and appreciation goes to my church family, Life Renewal Charismatic Church, for your total and complete trust, your prayer, support, encouragement, and the atmosphere of worship and prayer culture created in our church family, which inspired me to write this book. Lastly, to many others who supported, prayed, believed, and encouraged me to write this book, I say God bless you, and may this piece of work be a blessing in the kingdom in which we serve to the glory of God our King.

Introduction

I HAVE BEEN TAKEN BY IMMENSE SENSE OF URGENCY, THE importance of prayer in our journey as believers. Generally, many Christians have been struggling in this area of communication with God and have lost the inspiration of the spiritual benefits of prayer which yield physical fruits. The Holy of Holies, a small room that is built 10 cubits by 10 cubits, separated from the Holy place, which housed the most important redemptive piece of treasure to Israel's history, the Ark of the Covenant. There was neither sun nor artificial light, but God's *"Shekinah"* glory that lit up the Holy of Holies. There is no form of seat in the chamber except God's own seated glory. In addition, the Holy of Holies is a direct representation of heaven, that is, the throne room of the grace of God. When you come into your prayer chamber, you are supernaturally in the Holy of Holies, right in the presence of God. Many Christians underestimate the seriousness of standing in the presence of God. As a matter of fact, many dampen it down by placing less emphasis on the spiritual order of protocol, thereby underestimating the presence of God. Those who haven't grown in their walk with God lack a personal communion with

God. Most Christians today don't have a personal devotion with God. Ministers of the gospel have sufficed to ministerial appointments, conferences, programs, preaching, etc., in place of their personal devotional time with God.

A lot of us today "**know about**" God: This means we have studied and heard and have been given orientations, seminars, sermons, teaching "**about**" this God we claim to serve. However, it is time to "**know HIM.**" Knowing God is experiencing the LORD in the divine way: talking to Him, abiding in Him, walking with Him, serving and pleasing Him. Knowing God is about knowing who you are in HIM. In John 15:4, Jesus says,

> *"Abide in Me, and I in you. As the branch cannot bear fruit of itself, unless it abides in the vine, neither can you, unless you abide in Me."*

Therefore, this book is to open our eyes about the importance and benefits of experiencing our LORD in a true way in our daily life and walk with Him.

CHAPTER I

Power of Prayer

What is prayer? It is mankind giving God the license to interfere in earthly affairs. When we look at the origin of prayer, we see that the legal authority on earth is mankind. Genesis 1:26: "Then God said, 'Let us man in our image, according to our likeness: <u>let them have dominion over the fish of the sea, over the birds of the air, and over the cattle, over all the earth and over every creeping thing that creeps on earth.'" God created parts of mankind's existence on earth. First, God made the "man," which is the spirit from eternity, and placed it in a physical suit called "humus." The word "humus" means soil or dirt. Thus, the two components put together, God made the "human" or in our lay term, "human being."

Notice that God gave the position of dominion of physical things to humans as legal guardians. Therefore, as God is bound to His word, any spirit without a physical suit is an illegal citizen of earth. This is the reason why Satan needed the physical suit of the serpent to legally deal with humans. Psalms 115:16 says, "The heaven, even the heavens, are the LORD's; But the earth He has given to the children of men." Prayer is a pivotal and essential tool of power in the hand of mankind.

Prayer is meant to line us up in His will and with His empowerment. Faithfulness in prayer is the essential mechanism for reaching others with the faith. Nothing of value can accrue in you or through you without prayer. Prayer is our key to God's door. It is our foundation for exercising and growing in the faith and essential in our witnessing. It is the work of Christ through the work of the Spirit that saves. Prayer lines us up to His will and grows us in maturity and understanding. It is the power that encompasses the faith. To be effective in your growth in Christ, you have to be a person who prays—and prays regularly. If you think that you do not know how to pray, you need to ask yourself, *Do I know how to talk and listen?* If you do, then you know how to pray! Prayer is basically our communication with the Great, Sovereign God of the Universe, who wants the best for us and who wants to hear from us. The great wonder is not so much in how we pray, but that God is willing to listen to us. The great, wonderful *fallout* from our redemption is our ability to pray real and effective prayers that God actually hears and to which He responds. God will actually speak to us through His Word; the Holy Spirit will teach and convict us through the Word. The fact is, our prayer time with God is basically a conversation with Him, through which we express our gratitude for who He is, what He did for us, and how we can discover our purpose in life. Thus, through our prayers, we can be taught, grow, and be convicted so we can apply His precepts to our lives and affect those around us too. This then transfers to the people God lays upon our heart to reach, connecting with Him before we connect with them.

Purpose of Prayer

In Proverbs 19:21, it says, "Many are the plans in a person's heart, but it is the LORD's <u>purpose</u> that prevails."

The word "purpose" is defined as an original intent or the motivation for which something was created or made. In other words, your existence on earth is purposeful and never random. God is more concerned about HIS purpose for your life than your plans for yourself. Purpose always precedes plans, and that is to say, if you don't know why you do something, you will abuse it or destroy it.

It is interesting to note that the smallest meeting in church is a prayer meeting, which is also the smallest in our lives. This is because we consider prayer for a few intercessors. Note as it is made clear in the Bible, recorded in 1 Thessalonians 5:17, "Pray without ceasing."

The reason why we are not interested in prayer is because we don't get results and we don't have personal prayer lives.

Jesus, in His earthly ministry, never prayed with His disciples. Luke 11:1: "One day Jesus was praying in a certain place. When he finished, one of his disciples said to him, 'Lord, teach us to pray, just as John taught his disciples,' and Jesus said to them, 'And when you pray…'"

Notice that Jesus didn't say "And *if* you pray." This underlines grammatical truth: "If" is a conditional clause used for an uncertain occurrence of an event. It dwells on feelings or changes to the favor of the fact. "When" is used for a certainty of an event occurrence. Therefore, Jesus is stating that prayer is neither a choice nor an option. Prayer is a rather demanded activity that constantly connects us to the realm of the supernatural with our Father.

Maybe you are bothered by some questions which impede prayer. For instance, we ask, if God is sovereign, why pray? Or, if God is not influenced by me, why pray? Or, if God cannot be affected by what we say, then why pray? These questions have answers! God is as sovereign as HIS Word. In other words, HIS will doesn't exceed what HE has already said. This means God is limited by HIS Word and HE will never violate HIS Word.

I have a question for you: Do you frantically go about all your tasks of the day? Maybe you get stressed out. Do you get angry?

Do you think, *I will just keep going and going*? Or think, *Once I have dealt with all this stuff, I will start planning a better life*? No matter who you are, we are all subject to being overly busy. Students say they are too busy. Parents and workers say they are too busy. Even retired people are saying they are busy.

Managing directors of major businesses say one of the problems we all need to deal with is that being busy will come naturally and we are fools when we think that being busy is the most important thing for us and others. Now it is easy to be constantly caught up in the cycle of being active. There is nothing wrong with being active; however, life involves more than just being active. We all need to take time away from the busyness to plan, to prioritize, and to recharge. Getting away from busyness is not something we should feel guilty about.

In fact, getting away from busyness each day will help us see and deal with our busy and often complex lives.

The Bible says in Mark 1:35-37, *"Now in the morning, having risen a long while before daylight, He went out and departed to a solitary place; and there He prayed. And Simon and those who were with Him searched for Him. When they found Him, they said to Him, 'Everyone is looking for you.'"*

Jesus's busyness was not a bad thing, and often our busyness is not bad. But the problem is when we allow our busyness to dominate our lives, to overtake who we are and what we are doing. Our busyness causes us to neglect ourselves and especially neglect our relationship with God and other people. One of the things that I have to watch out for is that when I get too busy, it is easy to rush through Bible reading, to treat prayer as a routine, and during these times, the focus is often on me. Many people would have you believe that the best way to cope with busyness is to focus on yourself: to think about yourself first. Well, history tells us that such thinking will lead to more problems rather than less. Throughout the many years of Christianity, emphases have been placed on focusing only on ourselves. This leads to us experiencing not a better life, but a selfish, more sinful life. And that is the problem with many self-help books and gurus.

Some of them encourage us to think only of ourselves and to forget about others or at best to push others down the priority scale. The Bible says that Peter rose up looking for Jesus, and when he found him, he said, "Everyone is looking for you." The phrase "everyone is looking for you" is the world that we deal with every day when we set out of our homes. It is this demand from the world which locks us in a cycle of performance without a keen and precise impact. It is this moment that you get out of the busyness to seek the giver for the life and purpose of the day before you set your sights on the gifts.

We all have lists of things we would like to do in the next day, week, month, and even the next year. And certainly, there is nothing wrong with that. That is a good thing. But often, a goal that we miss is developing a deeper prayer life. Now, we all set aside a certain amount of time for God. For some, it is an enriching hour every day. But for most of us, sometimes the busyness of daily demands begins to crowd our time with God, and we buy into the lies that the enemy has placed in our lives toward prayer. C.S. Lewis wrote, "The moment you wake up each morning, all your wishes and hopes for the day rush at you like wild animals. And the first job each morning consists of shoving it all back, in listening to that other voice, taking that other point of view, letting that other, larger, stronger, quieter life come flowing in." I want you to understand that there is more work done in prayer than work itself. You see, when we allow the busyness of our lives to crowd in, our prayers can become vending-machine prayers. We quickly put in our money and punch in the numbers for what we want. A4-forgiveness, or D3-a good day, or C1-protection. It is a temptation to approach God from the **throne of race**, rather than meeting Him at the **throne of grace**.

Let us read Luke 10:38-42:

> *Now it happened as they went that He entered a certain village; and a certain woman named Martha welcomed Him into her house. And she had a sister called Mary, who also sat at Jesus' feet and heard His word. But Martha was distracted with much serving, and she approached Him and said, "Lord, do You not care that my sister has left me to serve alone? Therefore tell her to help me." And Jesus answered and said to her, "Martha, Martha, you are worried and troubled about many things. But one thing is needed, and Mary has chosen that good part, which will not be taken away from her."*

Seriously, this text gets me thinking, *What am I to do when I get an important guest, like the Son of God (Jesus), coming for dinner?* I think I will be running around to make dinner better than a two-minute cooked noodles and soup. So then, what is wrong with this scene in this text? What was Martha's problem? Was her desire to serve Jesus the problem? No, but we can see in verse forty that she was distracted. Martha was preoccupied with serving instead of sitting at Jesus's feet. She was also feeling sorry for herself. She says, "Lord, don't you care…?" And Martha was demanding. She tells the Lord what she wants Him to do, instead of letting the Lord tell her what to do. We get caught up in setting our own personal agenda before God, and we essentially move God into a box. The Bible says in Hebrews 4:16, *"Let us therefore come boldly to the throne of grace, that we may obtain mercy and find grace to help in time of need."* In other words, it is in the chambers where we can encounter God to refresh us and meet our need and strengthen us in our weaknesses. Prayer is a Christian's lifeline. A Christian life without prayer is like having a baby in your arms and dressing him/her up so cute—but he/she is not breathing! Never mind the frilly clothes; stabilize the child's vital signs. God desires a restored relationship with Him. If we have a relationship with Christ, then we are part of the family of God. We are brothers and sisters in Christ. But how can we go about or even know our Father's business if we don't talk to Him? I have to admit, it is far easier to run around and act Christian than to spend time with God in prayer. And I believe the enemy has cleverly worked his way into our attitudes of prayer. Perhaps he has some of us buying into the common lies he has placed within the Christian body: something is deemed successful if it produces results.

Lie number one of the enemy: Busy lives equal success, importance, and spirituality. Prayer doesn't always produce immediate results, so instead we should turn to busyness. It is easy to get caught up in being busy for God. God wants the fullness of life for us. But what does that mean? Does it mean, "God, I did this for You today? I went to work, and I did a good job? I helped out with the junior high today, and I managed to fix a bike today too. God, I'm doing a lot for you now. I'm busy teaching Sunday school, and on weekdays I coach hockey, and I see that we have this need here, and what about meeting with my friends, God? I need to be there for them, and I feel like I should get in shape so I will, and what about the children?!?! God, I'm really tired, but I was super busy. I'll spend time with You tomorrow." In filling our lives with activities, we end up missing the point: God wants us to pray to Him and meet with Him. It is then that our days get the fullest.

Another lie that Satan has subtly placed in our hearts is that prayer should be tried after all avenues have failed. The enemy's main strategy within the Christian body is, "Don't call, don't ask, and don't depend on God to do great things. You'll get along just fine if you rely on your own cleverness and energy." How many times this week have we scurried around, trying to make sure the kids were fed, friends were met, and jobs accomplished? And how many times, even in church settings, have we given lip service to God, asking for His blessing and went ahead with our own agendas? The Bible says in the book of *James 4:2, "You want something but don't get it. You kill and covet, but you cannot have what you want. You quarrel and fight. You do not have, because you do not ask God."* Not until we approach the throne of grace, which is the chambers, on our knees will we begin to see the Holy Spirit work in our lives and the world around us.

Collective prayer and devotion is important. However, the importance of personal prayer and intimacy with God is stressed in the Scriptures to be of a grave importance in our spiritual growth and journey with the LORD. Jesus said in the book of *Matthew 6:6, "But you, when you pray, go into your room, and when you have shut your door, pray to your Father who is in the secret place; and your Father who sees in secret will reward you openly."* I am sure that obedience to Christ's moral law and humility in how we see ourselves and others are both much more important, and no doubt there are other more important things in the bigger picture. Without obedience to Christ, you don't have a Christian experience, and if you have a proud view of yourself and your abilities, God will resist you. All the devotions in the world will not help you if you don't cast off your pride.

The Value of Prayer

Everything God is and has is available to mankind through prayer. It does not just happen, and the access is through prayer. Note that God needs you, and nothing will happen on earth without mankind. Therefore, without God, mankind cannot, and without mankind, God will not do anything on earth. We exist on earth with a secret legal power. When mankind began to lock out God from earthly affairs, we set ourselves on a collision course. In Genesis 3, when Adam and Eve locked out God through disobedience, they witnessed the first murder of their son Abel by the hand of their firstborn son, Cain. I want you understand that God depends on prayer to act in our affairs.

2 Chronicles 7:14 says, *"**If** My people who are called by My name will humble themselves, and pray and seek my face, and turn from their wicked ways, <u>then I will</u> hear from heaven and will forgive their sin and heal their land."* We can see that God uses dependency terms for prayer.

The Golden Censer

There is a powerful occurrence and manifestation during your prayer time. The Bible says in *Revelation 8:2-6,*

> *And I saw the seven angels who stand before God and to them were given seven trumpets. ³ Then another angel, having a golden censer, came and stood at the altar. He was given much incense that he should offer it with the prayers of all the saints upon the golden altar which was before the throne. And the smoke of the incense, with the prayers of the saints, ascended before God from the angel's hand. Then the angel took the censer, filled it with fire from the altar, and threw it to the earth. And there were noises, thunderings, lightnings, and an earthquake. So the seven angels who had the seven trumpets prepared themselves to sound.*

The censer was a copper bowl used for carrying coals and for burning incense, hence the word "censer." It was used in Old Testament days by the high priest to carry incense into the holiest of all on his annual visit there. Vials were bowls too and were broad and shallow, often used for incense and drink offerings. The word "vial" is used only in Revelation and then some eight times. In Revelation 5, the dramatic events witnessed by John reach their climax when no one is found worthy to open the scroll which was written within and on the back side. No room is available for further writing on this scroll, indicative of the fact that the whole counsel of God had already been defined and committed to writing. Nothing could happen to deflect or delay the program, and there is no opportunity to include things unforeseen, which is of course quite correct, as nothing is unforeseen as far as God is concerned. The scroll lays in God's right hand, indicating that the next stage of the divine plan is about to unfold, provided a way can be found to open it.

However, no one is found worthy to open the book, and John weeps at this apparent hitch in the divine plan. It is then announced that the Lion of the tribe of Judah had prevailed to open the book and to unlock the seven seals. Learning this, John expects to see a Lion but is surprised to see a Lamb as it had been slain, but now in the majesty and power of victory.

As the Lamb takes the scroll, the twenty-four elders fall down before Him and sing a new song, the glorious words of which are recorded in this chapter. It should also be noted that the elders each have a harp and a golden bowl containing incense odors—the prayers of saints. As they gather around the standing Lamb, they fall down and worship Him—yet a sad reminder of those earthly elders in Jerusalem who had gathered round only to mock and to reject His claims. The harp is the first musical instrument referred to in the Bible and the only one mentioned as being used in heaven. That the elders should have harps is unsurprising, but they also carry golden bowls. In these bowls are many odors, described as being the prayers of saints. Thus, praise and prayer unite in an appreciation of the Lamb.

Prayers are precious to God—just as they will be then, have been in the past, so they are today. These bowls of prayers are golden—precious, weighty, broad, and are in God's presence at the very point of decision where angels wait ready to do His bidding. They are available to fly immediately at His command to answer prayer. WOW! Can you imagine the intense activity in the throne room of grace when prayers are offered? It is amazing to fathom how heaven's activities rely on earthly prayers of the saints. Let us continue to pray in the certain knowledge that God hears, cares, and is always ready to intervene in favor of His people. As we read from Revelation 8, it opens with silence in heaven for the space of half an hour, prior to the opening of the seventh and final seal of the scroll. This is not the sweet silence of rest and peace, but the ominous silence as of the calm before the storm. It lasts but a short time, half an hour, but the depth of the silence and its heavy atmosphere make it seem to be very much longer indeed. After this period of silence, the seven angels are each given a trumpet with which to officially announce the judgements of God.

Now another Angel appears standing at the altar and having a golden censer. To this Angel, none other than our Lord Jesus Christ is given much incense. Here, the incense speaks of the beauties of His character and life, which His sufferings brought out in full fragrance. The incense of Old Testament days was made up of four parts and was very precious and holy. The ingredients were stacte, onycha, galbanum, and frankincense, perfectly balanced, tempered together, pure, and holy. Beaten very small, it was placed before the Ark of the Covenant, where God met man. This beautiful incense is now to be mingled with the prayers of the saints, and together they are offered to God. These particular prayers are of course for judgement, but whether for judgement or mercy, the beauty of Christ in all His perfection, as appreciated by God, is mingled with the prayers of saints. Not just added to but mingled with, so that the life of Christ and His sufferings are an indistinguishable part of the prayers. No wonder Satan trembles when he sees the weakest saint upon their knees! Glory to God!!...Satan is powerless when you get on your knees in prayer because this activity conveys a supernatural verdict and indictment against the powers of darkness.

Having offered the incense and prayers from His hand, the Angel then fills the golden bowl with fire and, in a dramatic gesture of judicial judgement, casts the fire of God into the earth. This fire too (like the incense) has four parts, voices, thundering, lightning, and an earthquake, after which the seven angels sound their trumpets, in turn initiating judgments the like of which earth has never before experienced. The prayers are answered at once! Prayer is a powerful weapon when used, as against enemies in that day, or for the good of those for whom we intercede. Let us continue in prayer in the knowledge that to all our prayer and praises Christ adds His sweet perfume, and love the censer raises their odors to consume. Thus, these golden bowls of Revelation teach us that the prayers of saints are highly valued in heaven and lie at His right hand, ready to be acted on immediately. Secondly, that the prayers of saints are always mingled with the beauty and acceptability of their Lord and as such are irresistible. Thirdly, that the prayers and incense finally give way to wrath and fury, which are poured out on earth in such a way that is unstoppable until God is satisfied that the demands of His throne and sanctuary have been fully met.

Golden censers and vials play a vital role in future events yet can be used to our advantage in a personal way.

Chapter II

The Presence of God

The word "environment" is defined as circumstances, objects, and conditions by which one is surrounded. Therefore, an environment may refer to the forces that affect the state of things. In the principles of environment, everything in life is created to function within the particular surroundings that God prescribed for it before creation. God made everything based on the environment created for the very existence of that creation. In other words, before God spoke plants and animals into being, He gathered the waters together so that dry ground would appear. The dry ground God called "land" and the waters He called "seas." Only then did God speak to the sea, commanding it to bring forth the many kinds of fish and sea creatures. Therefore, with this example of God's systematic level of creation, no matter how expensive the creation or product is, it will shut down if the environment of operation is different from what the creator intended. In other words, a wrong environment for a creation will be translated into wasted potential.

Psalms 1:1-3 says, "[1] Blessed is the one who does not walk in step with the wicked or stand in the way that sinners take or sit in the company of mockers, ² but whose delight is in the law of the LORD, and who meditates on his law day and night. ³ That person is like a tree planted by streams of water, which yields its fruit in season and whose leaf does not wither—whatever they do prosper." The Bible says, "Blessed is the man…" This word literally means "happy, completely satisfied, or blissful." If you are saved, you have God living inside you. We must understand this. Psalms 16:11 says, "¹¹ You make known to me the path of life; you will fill me with joy in your presence, with eternal pleasures at your right hand." However, if Jesus were with us twenty-four hours a day, seven days a week, would your life change? If the answer is yes, you must realize that Jesus is with us always and walks with us through life. We have all the privileges of friendship with God: we can speak to Him in prayer; He speaks to us in His Word and by the assurance of His Spirit in our hearts. We can seek His advice, share our worries, and ask Him for help. We can tell Him our joys and our sorrows. Our relationship with the Lord is even closer than face to face, because God's Spirit actually lives in us. We don't need to go out to a tent, to a church, or to the top of a mountain. We can meet with the Lord every day, every minute, everywhere. It's a fantastic privilege, isn't it?!

The presence of God in our lives is one of the great attributes of our lives. A Christian cannot do without the presence of God. In the Holy of Holies, the Ark of the Covenant is placed at the center of the room, and the top of the ark is designed to sit the two cherubim facing each other and their wings touching each other. It is between these cherubim that the presence of God shines in a radiant light more than the sun.

In this description, I am talking about the manifest presence of God. God's manifest presence is a special anointing for a special task at a specific time. It is temporal in nature. His power will flow in a meeting, touching the lives of people, healing many, and delivering others from the power of the enemy. During the dedication of the temple we read in **2 Chronicles 5:13, 14,** "**...*then the house of the Lord was filled with a cloud, so that the priests could not stand to minister because of the cloud, for the glory of the Lord filled the house of the Lord.*"** In Acts 9:3-4, we read of Saul's encounter with the manifest presence of the Lord that changed even his name! "*As he traveled on he came near to Damascus and suddenly a light from heaven flashed around him and he fell to the ground. Then he heard a voice saying to him: Saul, Saul why are you persecuting me?*" When Jesus prayed on the mountain, He was transfigured as the manifest presence came down (Luke 9:29). This manifest presence engulfs your very being while you are in the chamber of holy of holies with God.

In Psalm 15, David begins with a question in verse 1, which he answers in the verses that follow: "Lord, who may dwell in your sanctuary? Who may live on your holy hill?" The question which David poses has to do with living in the presence of God. "How may I as your child live daily in your presence?" David asks. The reason he asks this question is that he understands well the power that comes to one's life when they live with a daily awareness of the presence of God.

David's understanding of the power of God's presence is illustrated by the way he phrases his question.

David understood that living with the realization of God's presence in one's life has the power to:

A. Provide a sense of direction in life:

The word for "sanctuary" literally means "tent" and refers to the tent that David pitched for the Ark of the Covenant to be placed in.

A tent is a symbol for something transient and temporary. A tent is easily struck; it is a moveable house, the very symbol of pilgrimage in the Old Testament. Abraham, Isaac, and Jacob lived in tents, although they were wealthy men and could easily have built palaces to live in instead. They were content, however, to live in tents so that they might be ready to move in a moment's notice at the call of God.

Likewise, we must realize that our lives are transient and temporary. If we are going to make the most of the time we have in this life, we must pursue God's presence, knowing that as we do, we will have His guidance and direction. Living daily with an awareness of the presence of God provides us with a sense of direction in our pilgrimage on earth.

B. Provide a sense of security in life:

A hill is a symbol for something permanent. Indeed, David's desire was not for the Ark of the Covenant to be kept forever in a tent. He wanted to eventually house the ark in a temple on mount Moriah.

In speaking of the "holy hill" of God, David was referring to the fact that living daily with an awareness of God's presence in my life provides me with a sense of security concerning one day being with the Lord in heaven.

Living life with a daily awareness of God's presence allows us to be directed in our pilgrimage here on earth and to be secured in our expectation of being with God one day in heaven.

Well, how can I live with a daily awareness of God's presence? Let's note what David tells us here about the characteristics of one who persists in the presence of God.

The first thing David talks about is his walk: if one is going to dwell daily in the Lord's presence, his walk must be "blameless." The background of the word used here for "blameless" is most interesting. If an Old Testament worshipper wanted to bring a special burnt offering to God, he would find a full-grown ram, one of his prize breeding stocks, the very best in his flock, to offer. He would run his hand and eye over it to make sure that it had no hidden blemish. He would take it to the priest, who would also give it a careful examination. The ram would then be slain, and the priest would expose all of its inward parts, sharply watching out for any imperfection. Only a perfect sacrifice was acceptable to be offered to God.

It is this process of examination to which this word "blameless" refers. That which David tells us here then, is that if one is going to dwell daily in the reality of the Lord's presence, he must examine himself daily to make sure there is nothing in his life that would cause him to be "unclean" in the sight of God, as is stated in the book of 1 Corinthians 11:28, "But let a man examine himself, and so let him eat of the bread and drink of the cup." Taking things a step further, we must also insist that just as the sacrifice of the Old Testament worshipper was examined not only by the worshipper, but also by the priest, we must be careful to not only examine our lives daily, but to allow our Great High Priest, Jesus, to examine our lives daily, as the book of Psalms 139:23-24 says, "Search me, O God, and know my heart; Try me, and know my anxieties; And see if *there is any* wicked way in me, And lead me in the way everlasting." A wonderful contrast to note is that while the Old Testament animal would be rejected upon discovery of a blemish, you and I, upon discovery of any blemish of sin in our lives, can submit to the cleansing of our Great High Priest. A member of a major non-Christian religion said to a missionary to India, "Tell me one thing your religion can offer the people of India that mine can't." The missionary thought for a moment and replied, "Forgiveness! Forgiveness!"

Unlike the followers of all other world religions, those who put their hope in Christ have full assurance that their sins are forgiven. British Bible teacher David Pawson says, "I have talked to devout Muslims who pray five times a day, have journeyed to Mecca, have fasted during Ramadan, and are more devout than many Christians. But when I ask, 'Do you know if your sins are forgiven?' they've said, 'We don't. We just have to hope for the best.'"

The Christian who daily enjoys the reality of God's presence in his life is one who subjects himself to examination daily, thereby making sure that his walk before the Lord is blameless.

The second point David talks about is his work: if one is going to dwell daily in the Lord's presence, his work must be "righteous." Righteous works are works that are "right." How can I know I am doing the "right" things? Through obedience to the revealed will of God for my life, as is stated in the book of Ephesians 2:10, "For we are His workmanship, created in Christ Jesus for good works, which God prepared beforehand that we should walk in them." One who enjoys a daily awareness of God's presence in his life is one who has made being right with God and doing right for God a daily priority. In other words, his desire is only to please God! He lives for an audience of one! John McKay was, for many years, the worship leader for the James Robinson evangelistic association, until the ministry took a new direction. Afterwards, he and his ministry fell into relative obscurity.

He says that in a moment when he was feeling sorry for himself, he walked to the back part of his property in Texas. He sat down on the side of a hill and saw below him a beautiful field of bluebonnets in full bloom.

He said to the Lord, "Lord, why have you put these bluebonnets on the back side of my property, where I have never seen them? Why not put them out in the front of our property, where we and others passing by might enjoy them?" And he said he heard God speak to his heart and say, "I didn't put them there for your enjoyment or anyone else's. I put them there for me." We exist to please HIM and not ourselves.

The third point David talks about is his words: if one is going to dwell daily in the Lord's presence, his words must be "fitting." James 1:26, says, *"If anyone among you thinks he is religious, and does not bridle his tongue but deceives his own heart, this one's religion is useless."* The reality of the Lord's presence in our lives will have a "double-edged" effect upon our speech. To maintain an awareness of God's presence, one should be careful not to sin in what they say, and because of their awareness of God's presence, they will want to be careful not to sin in what they say!

The fourth point David talks about is his ways: if one is going to dwell daily in the Lord's presence, his ways must be "pure." In other words, his motives will be pure: he will not be out to get ahead at the expense of others. Instead, he will be sincerely concerned about helping others in whatever way the Lord would enable him to do so. His methods will be pure: he will not be the kind of person who does anything to get ahead in life. Instead, he will seek to be a person of integrity who draws the line when it comes to conducting their business in life.

When it comes to the way in which he conducts himself, the person who is preoccupied with God's presence in his life will be more concerned with integrity than with image! He will be more concerned about how he is viewed by God above than by the world.

David concludes this Psalm by saying of the person who persists in the presence of God that he will never be shaken. Why? Because he will live his life with a sense of direction from God and with a sense of security in God!

Dwelling in the Presence

When electricity became available in remote rural areas, one woman went to great trouble and expense to have electricity installed in her home. A few months after the wiring was installed and the power was turned on, the power company noticed that the home didn't use very much power. Fearing that there was a problem, they sent a meter reader to check on the matter. The meter reader saw that the power was indeed working properly and then asked the woman, "Do you use your electricity?" The woman replied, "Of course we do. We turn it on every night to see to light our lamps and then we turn it off."

Doesn't that just sound ridiculous, having all of the power that you need and the ability to tap it all the time but only using it just enough to "get by"? We would never do anything like this because it just wouldn't make sense. However, we do this same thing a great deal when we apply the same reasoning to the power and presence of God. We go out of our way to go to church and to worship but have little relationship with God through the week. We go through difficulties day after day, and only when we come to the end of our strength do we ask for God's help. We have the power of God at our disposal all of the time, but yet we attempt to get by on our own strength every day. We are a lot more like the woman who wouldn't use her electricity than we would like to admit.

We need to experience the presence of God to experience His power. Just like electricity, when we remove the presence of God from our lives, we also remove the power.

God created all of humanity to have a deep personal relationship with Him. God literally walked with Adam and Eve in the Garden of Eden. Think about that for a moment. Let it sink in. God walked and talked with Adam and Eve. They were able to completely enjoy His divine presence. God's desire for your life is to have that same kind of relationship with Him. He wants you to be able to walk in His presence.

Moses speaks with God in Exodus 33:12-23 and simply reminds God of His promises. Why does Moses do this? It is not like God forgot the promises He made. Moses has a genuine concern here. God had removed His presence from the Israelite camp! There was no longer a sense of the divine within the nation of Israel. How often do we feel the same way about church but are too afraid to say it? How many come into the sanctuary week after week having no experience with God? What is the problem?

We are not seeking more of God. We settle for the status quo and leave our lives there. If we settle with what we have already experienced with God, we cannot grow. When we settle for where we are with God, we will never move forward in our walk with Him. The truth is that we cannot simply settle anymore! When Moses sought God, he did so through fervent prayer. He sought God by going on his knees. One of the biggest problems in the church today is that people want a deep relationship with God but don't want to pay the price for it. Developing an intimate relationship with God takes time and effort. It doesn't happen overnight. Therefore, make it your daily priority to live in HIS presence.

Chapter III

Child of God

To be a child of God, our faith must be a faith that will accept and do all that the Lord tells us to do. It must be an obedient faith, because God says in James 2:17, 20, and 24, "Thus also faith, by itself, if it does not have works, is dead." "But do you want to know, O foolish man, that faith without works is dead?" "You see then that a man is justified by works, and not by faith only." We are not saved by "faith only." If our faith is not one of action, it is a dead faith. Therefore, the only currency accepted in the kingdom to trade for heavenly treasures is faith.

In medical terms, a child bares the Deoxyribose Nucleic Acid (DNA) composition of the father. In other words, the characteristics of the father define the lifestyle of the child. Jesus, being the Son of God, is always connected to the Father for guidance and direction. In lay terms, A son who has many siblings but isn't close to the father always asks his siblings about what their father thinks and plans for him, whether the father is upset with him or loves him, whether the father plans to give him some of the inheritance or not. Such a child always has a mindset of a biased father who loves some and hates some.

The Bible says in *Luke 15:20-24,*

> *So he got up and went to his father. But while he was still a long way off, his father saw him and was filled with compassion for him; he ran to his son, threw his arms around him and kissed him. The son said to him, "Father, I have sinned against heaven and against you. I am no longer worthy to be called your son." But the father said to his servants, "Quick! Bring the best robe and put it on him. Put a ring on his finger and sandals on his feet. Bring the fattened calf and kill it. Let's have a feast and celebrate. For this son of mine was dead and is alive again; he was lost and is found." So they began to celebrate.*

The parable is a very familiar one, and it is full of sacred meaning that always has some fresh lesson for us. Let us then consider the antecedents to this kissing. On the son's side there was something, and on the father's side much more. Before the prodigal son received these kisses of love, he had said in the far country, "I will arise and go to my father." He had, however, done more than that, else his father's kiss would never have been upon his cheek. The resolve had become a deed: "He arose, and came to his father." A blushful of resolutions is of small value; a single grain of practice is worth the whole. The determination to return home is good, but it is when the wandering boy begins the business of really carrying out the good resolve that he draws near the blessing.

True Identity

Our identity, our true personhood, all begins with God, God's love, and God's grace, which has made us who and what we are. The book of *1 John 3:1 says, "See what love the Father has given us, that we should be called children of God; and that is what we are."* For John then, there can be no greater status, no finer identity, than being called and named by God through His love and grace as CHILD OF GOD. As the writer goes on to explain, our identity, our true personhood, is inseparable from how we live as Christians.

Phrenologists claim that they can tell what type of a person you are, or will be, by the bumps on your skull. Graphologists claim they can read your character through your handwriting. Physiognomists claim that they can read your character by the shape of your nose, the set of your jaw, the texture of your skin.

These are complicated ways of judging a person's character, but I would like to tell you a quicker method. Find out the consuming passion of a person's life, their greatest love. Is it the love of money? Then no matter what the subject of the conversation, it will come back to money matters again and again. Or is it love of gossip? Then it will show on the face, and the eyes will sparkle at some spicy comment made about another. I could go on, for everyone takes on something of the countenance of the thing they love most. Those of us who are parents know how the identities of our children grow out of our relationship with them. Children, especially when they are young, love to imitate their parents. They often try to talk and act the same way they see their parents talking and acting. As we all know, this can be a humbling as well as inspiring experience for us—since our children pick up both our bad and good habits. John is telling us the same is true for us as Christians. Our identity, says John, is influenced by fixing our lives on Christ. As children of God, we become more Christlike by following or imitating Christ's words and actions. One of the words John uses in this passage to highlight the importance of our identity being rooted in Christ is the word "see." For John, how we Christians SEE Christ is very important. Why is this so? Well, many biblical scholars believe that one of the groups that were influencing John's faith community was the Gnostics. They were teaching something very different about Jesus than what John was teaching. The Gnostics believed that matter and therefore the physical human body was not important. What was really important was the soul. Therefore, the way one lived in this world really did not matter, since matter and the body had no influence on the soul. A person could do whatever they pleased; whether it was good or bad, it made no difference. Therefore, for the Gnostics, Jesus really did not come as the Savior to suffer and die on a cross for our sins.

John responds to this Gnostic view by emphasizing that Jesus did come into the world to suffer and die for our sins and what we do with our physical bodies does matter. Therefore, John was instructing his community not to follow the example of what they saw the Gnostics doing. Rather, they are to follow the example of what they saw Christ Himself do and accomplish for them.

Image is latent on a film; it requires development to draw out the picture. We too have potential as children of God. However, we too need development and the proper process to make it plain and useable. We are, for as long as we live, WORKS IN PROGRESS. The work of the Holy Spirit in us and through us is always ongoing. So, we continue to grow in our journey of faith as children of God.

Royal Priesthood

There are two basic types of people who call themselves Christians: those who seek after a preacher to tickle their ears with warm and fuzzy sermons, and those who work to develop a strong servant relationship with Jesus Christ. It all depends on where their minds are focused. We can focus on our earthly life, or we can focus on the kingdom of God. It is kind of like the story of Nicodemus. Back during the time of Jesus's earthly ministry, there was a man named Nicodemus; he was an important Jewish religious leader and a Pharisee. He was very knowledgeable and should have recognized the truth about Jesus, but he was too focused on his earthly life to understand Jesus's teachings.

After dark one evening, Nicodemus came to speak with Jesus. "Rabbi," he said, "we all know that God has sent you to teach us. Your miraculous signs are evidence that God is with you."

Now, Jesus simply replied, "I tell you the truth, unless you are born from above, you cannot see the kingdom of God."

"What do you mean?" exclaimed Nicodemus. "How can an old man go back into his mother's womb and be born again?"

Jesus calmly replied, "I assure you, no one can enter the kingdom of God without being born of water and the Spirit. Humans reproduce human life, but the Holy Spirit gives birth to spiritual life. So, don't act so surprised when I say, 'If you are to have a spiritual life you must be born from above: be born again.' Look at it this way, the wind blows wherever it wants; you can hear the wind but you can't tell where it comes from or where it is going. It is the same with being born again; you can't explain how people are born of the Spirit."

This answer did not satisfy Nicodemus, and he asked, "How are these things possible?"

Jesus just could not let this opportunity pass, so He replied, "You are a respected Jewish teacher, and yet you don't understand these things?" This hit the Pharisee right between the eyes. While Nicodemus was still reeling from the last explanation, Jesus went on to say, "Let me remind you, when we tell you what we know and have seen you ignore us and won't believe our testimony. Therefore, if you don't believe me when I tell you about earthly things, how can you possibly believe if I tell you about heavenly things? Don't you realize that no one has ever gone to heaven and returned? No one that is, but the Son of Man who has come down from heaven. And as Moses lifted up the bronze snake on a pole in the wilderness, so the Son of Man must be lifted up, so that everyone who believes in him will have eternal life." It was being made very clear to Nicodemus that Jesus had the heavenly knowledge, authority, and power to explain being born again, but the earthly-minded Nicodemus could not understand. (John 3:1-21)

It is the same today: a disciple of Jesus Christ has the heavenly knowledge, authority, and power to explain being born again, but many people will not let themselves understand. Their mortal minds do not want to hear that the Law of the First Covenant illuminated sin and gave it the power to condemn all of mankind, but Jesus took our guilt upon Himself and crucified it, covering it with His own blood. Now, there is no judgment against anyone who believes in Jesus. But anyone who does not believe in Him has already been judged for not believing in God's only Son. And the judgment is based on this fact: God's light came into the world, but people loved the darkness more than the light, for their actions were evil. Therefore, those who are lost are not condemned because of their sins, but because they have disobeyed God and rejected Jesus Christ. Their sins are a physical manifestation of their evil nature, which is proven by their failing to bow their knee to the supreme deity of Christ. In fact, all who are disobedient to God automatically hate the light and refuse to go near it for fear their sins will be exposed. But those who do what is right come to the light so others can see that they are doing what God wants. That is why, if you are born again, you strive to do what is right and you cannot stand for sin to reign in your bodies. This is not to say we never sin, but we never allow sin to rule over us and generate in us a sinful lifestyle. If we are to mature, we will avoid those who keep going over the same basic teachings about Christ…again and again. Instead, we must go on and become mature in our understanding. What good does it do for those who are truly born again to constantly repeat training in the fundamental importance of repenting from evil deeds and placing our faith in God? If you are born from above, you need to close your earthly eyes so that you can see with the spirit and behold all the living stones: all those who are born again. Look, God is building His spiritual temple with all these living stones and with Jesus Christ as the chief cornerstone. What's more, we are the holy priests in this spiritual temple. And as royal priests, we offer spiritual sacrifices, which please God, through our worship of Jesus Christ.

As the Scriptures say, "I am placing a cornerstone in Jerusalem, chosen for great honor, and anyone who trusts in him will never be disgraced." (1 Peter 2:6). Yes, you who trust Him recognize the honor God has given Him. But for those who reject Him, "the stone that the builders rejected has now become the cornerstone." (Psalm 118:22) And, "He is the stone that makes people stumble, the rock that makes them fall." (1 Peter 2:8). They stumble because they do not obey God's word; they reject the cornerstone, and so they meet the fate that was planned for them. But we are not like that, for we are a chosen people. We are royal priests, a holy nation, and God's very own possession. As a result, we can show others the goodness of God, for He called us out of the darkness into His wonderful light. "Once you had no identity as a people; now you are God's people. Once you received no mercy; now you have received God's mercy." (1 Peter 2:10). We serve Jesus Christ, as His Royal Priesthood, in the Holy Temple built with living stones. As a royal priest, you must constantly offer sacrifices of praise, worship, and intercession to King Jesus. Nevertheless, we Christians have been chosen as God's ambassadors, charged to "proclaim the excellences of Him who called us out of darkness into His marvelous light." (1 Peter 2:9). Our position is not simply that of redeemed individuals, though we are indeed delivered from condemnation; we are declared heirs of Heaven and co-heirs with Jesus Christ. I would never depreciate the privilege that we enjoy because of His grace. However, I must emphasize that privilege always confers responsibility. Our enjoyment is not God's primary concern; rather, His righteous desire is the glory that accrues to Him through bringing many souls to life.

Christians are designated a royal priesthood. Each Christian is a priest, appointed by God, serving to petition Him for those individuals living in the world and serving as Christ's representative in the world. We are called by God and appointed by Him to stand between Him and fallen man. It is God's will that each Christian endeavor to bring the lost to faith in the Son of God. We do this through praying for their salvation and testifying to the grace of God.

Chapter IV

Seek and You Shall Find

The Bible says in the book of Hebrews 11:6, "⁶But without faith *it is* impossible to please *Him,* for he who comes to God must believe that He is, and *that* He is a rewarder of those who diligently seek Him."

We can see the Hebrew writer intuitively stating that God rewards those who long to know HIM and to please HIM. To diligently seek means to take painstaking efforts to look for something. In Greek, the translation for "diligently seek" is "*ekzeteo*" which means "to seek with more than a casual effort." In other words, energy, time, and resource are invested in the things that we know will pay out good dividend in our lives. For example, a student will "burn candle" in the night and go through the night without sleep to review the last couple of notes before the end-of-semester exam. The reason for this commitment is to get good grades. Similarly, there is a reward for those who seek diligently for the LORD. The Bible says in Jeremiah 29:13 that "…you will seek Me and find *Me,* when you search for Me with all your heart." When you seek the LORD with all your heart, it means HE is worth more than everything you have in this life. Jesus expounds seeking diligently for God in the book of Matthew 13:44, saying, *"The kingdom of heaven is like a treasure hidden in the field, which a man found and hid again; and from joy over it he goes and sells all that he has and buys that field."*

We meet a woman call Hannah who had a wonderful husband that loved her dearly. However, because of her childlessness, she felt incomplete and unfulfilled. *1 Samuel 1:10 says, "And she was in bitterness of soul, and prayed to the Lord and wept in anguish."* She went to God in prayer!! The Chamber brings you up close and personal with God, with the entire world outside: it is the prayer unspoken! Feeling incomplete or unfulfilled may be your story today—but take heart; tomorrow is coming. There is a sequel—with Jesus Christ as the author and finisher of your faith! Emily Dickinson wrote, "The world is not a conclusion; a sequel stands beyond, invisible as music, but positive as sound." (*Poem: This world is not a conclusion*)

God surely is the rewarder of those who diligently seek HIM. When you see the importance and the benefits that come with seeking the LORD, you will lay everything on the table every day to know HIM and please HIM.

If the "rewards" of this verse in Hebrews seem too remote to relate to, then pray that the Lord will give you the "spirit of revelation."

The book of Ephesians 1:15-19 says,

> *For this reason I too, having heard of the faith in the Lord Jesus which exists among you and your love for all the*

> *saints, do not cease giving thanks for you, while making mention of you in my prayers; that the God of our Lord Jesus Christ, the Father of glory, may give to you a* spirit of wisdom and of revelation *in the knowledge of Him. I pray that the eyes of your heart may be enlightened, so that you will know what is the hope of His calling, what are the riches of the glory of His inheritance in the saints, and what is the surpassing greatness of His power toward us who believe. These are in accordance with the working of the strength of His might.*

Until you begin to understand the "riches of the glory of his inheritance in the saints," you will not understand the concept of "diligently seek" or the concept of "sold all he had and bought the field."

Outside of your job, have you spent more time on worldly pursuits (TV, hobbies, family activities, relaxation, etc.) than you have pursuing God (Bible study, prayer, meditating on the Word, reading biblical material, listening to spiritually based messages, family study time or family fellowship time with God as the focus, etc.)?

Deep Longing

When you think about words, the word "down" doesn't have many positive meanings. It is a word reserved for cowards, losers, and bear markets. It is a word that is to be avoided or ignored. When you attach it to other words, it brings them down, such as "down and out," "down hearted," "downfall," "down-scale," "downhill," "downer," and "down under." Of course, what is worse for the word down is its opposite, "up."

The word "up" has many positive connotations. It is reserved for winners, heroes, and bull markets. Add the word "up" to other words and look what happens—"upscale," "up and coming," "upwardly mobile," "upper class," and "upstanding."

When we think about our present world, we have been deluged with the philosophy that our sights should be to move up in the world. It plays into our egos and delights us to no end. "Up" is a word that signifies one who has power. It is assumed that the direction of greatness is always up. Up, up, up! People rise against the odds; they ascend to fame and power.

Yet, with that in mind, the words of John the Baptist startle us. John tells his disciples, "Jesus must increase and I must decrease." (John

3:30). It would seem that the greatest oxymoron would be the phrase "descending into greatness." It seems absurd, yet that is exactly what John was saying to his disciples.

As we look at the yearning of our souls, what will it take to open the eyes of our hearts and souls and scream out to God to fill us, fill us until we cannot take it anymore? Have you ever laughed so hard that you could not take any more laughter? Have you gotten to the point of laughing so hard that your stomach hurts, your eyes are tearing? It feels so good, yet anymore laughter, and you think you will burst!

That is the type of filling in our souls and hearts I'm talking about. Not a cheap imitation, but the real thing. You see, we have a lot of choices out there. We can choose a lot of imitation or generic products. Some of them may make you think they are the real thing, but your soul knows the difference. In this instance, notice that the real butterscotch looks better and tasted better. By itself, it is an obvious choice. However, once you wrap that around some flour, sugar, vanilla, eggs, and make it into a dessert, it is much more difficult to tell which is the real one.

The same holds true in the world. When we stop and look at Jesus, we believe and are certain we should have all of Him. We should invite Jesus into our lives and submit ourselves to Him. And that is what God intended for us. Yet, we become so caught up in the world and all that it offers us, and pretty soon, we forget about "Jesus alone," and we become consumed with the desires of the world; and before we know it, everything becomes blended. We are not sure what is true and what is false. Everything has become so clouded, and in a strange way, we may find that we are comfortable. But that comfort lasts for only a short while, and we end up with a longing; and this time, it is even deeper than before.

Now we have a choice…do we go forward with reckless abandon and embrace Jesus, or do we settle for what we already have, simply because we know that this is far safer than grabbing hold of Jesus? Let me stop here and ask you, are you with me? Do you know what I mean about that choice? Because the deepest desires in our heart are predicated on what choices we make.

So now, let us look at John the Baptist for a few moments and see what we can learn from him.

This passage occurs immediately after Jesus's conversation with Nicodemus. During that conversation, Jesus told Nicodemus that he needed to be born again, and of course Jesus said the most famous verse in the Bible, John 3:16.

After that conversation, Jesus and His disciples traveled about fifty miles to an area called Salim. It was located along the Jordan River, and this is the only recording we have of Jesus baptizing people. John the Baptist was at the same place, baptizing people on the other side of the Jordan River. An argument developed between John's disciples and another Jewish man. We are not certain what it was about, but the end result was that John's disciples came back to John and questioned what Jesus was doing.

They told John, "That man who was with you on the other side of the Jordan—the one you testified about—well, he is baptizing, and everyone is going to him." (John 3:26). You see, these men were loyal followers of John the Baptist. Now this new guy comes into town, and they did not like it one bit. To them, it was competition. If you owned a store and it was the only one of its kind in town, and suddenly someone else opened a competing store, you may not be very excited about it.

Notice how John's disciples referred to Jesus. They don't call Him by name (Jesus), nor do they refer to Him as the Messiah, even though that is how John referred to Him. Instead, they speak of Jesus as "the one who was with you…the one you testified about." I believe they came to resent who Jesus was. His identity and His success are related. John knew who Jesus was; the disciples did not. John knew that it was time for Jesus to gain in popularity and for John to begin to diminish in popularity. But John's disciples did not understand what was going on, and frankly, they were jealous of Jesus's success. Notice that they told John, "Everyone is going to Jesus."

Now John explains to his disciples that he is not the Christ, but he was sent to come ahead of the Christ. John gives an illustration about a bride and groom. When the wedding came, it was the responsibility of the best man or best friend of the groom to take care of many of the details surrounding the wedding. The friend would act as a liaison between the man and the woman. In essence, the friend arranged the wedding, delivered invitations, and presided at the wedding feast, kind of like an MC. He also had one final duty, when it was time; he was to guard the bridal chamber so that no false lovers could get in. Once he saw the groom and heard his voice, he let the groom into the room.

Now the friend's job was over. This was a joyful job for the friend of the groom. He did not begrudge his friend; instead, there was joy in the completion of his task. His job was to bring the bride and groom together, and once that was accomplished, his job was to fade out of the picture.

John's disciples would understand that analogy. John's task was to bring Israel, the bride, and Jesus, the bridegroom, together. Now that this job was complete, John was happy to fade into the background. So, it was not with envy or bitterness that John said, "Jesus must increase and I must decrease." John would have said it with joy. Not with anger.

I truly believe that when we want to find the kingdom of God, when we want to find heaven, right here on earth, we must be willing to do exactly as John did. We must descend into greatness. I do not think there is any other way to do it. We cannot get there by going halfway. That will never work. You know, and so do I. But there are risks involved. The risk is that we must submit our lives and even surrender ourselves to God. We cannot give God just a little bit, like sticking your legs into the water, and that is all of God that you want. We must jump back in. For without jumping in, without giving all of ourselves to God, we will never experience the true joy, grace, peace, and love that God has in store for us. The risk is that we become more Christlike. And it is a risk because when we become more like Christ, we are faced with greater challenges. We are faced with fighting off the powers of evil, which are certain to come our way. The more we walk with Christ, the more Satan will throw our way. I am certain of that. We will have greater temptations, yet we will have greater joy when we resist those temptations.

The beauty of Christ increasing in our lives is the way we live our lives, it is the way we experience life, and it is the way others will see how we live life. When we have Christ increasing, our soul will be more satisfied, even in the midst of pain and suffering, trials, and tribulations. We will experience greater joy, greater love, greater peace, and greater grace. Others will look at us and marvel at how our spirit is so good. You must remain in the Chambers with God daily to ensure Christ increasing in your life. It is being humble when it may surprise others at our humility. I love it when athletes and other entertainers give thanks to God for their accomplishments. When it is done with sincerity, it is another example of a person who has decreased so God can increase. In the same way, coming to God daily satisfies the deep longing of God increasing in your life.

What longing do you have today that needs to be filled? Do not accept any imitations. There is only one way to fill our soul. Call on Jesus; if you must, get on your knees, fall face down on the ground, and humble yourself before the Lord. No matter how you do it, call on Jesus, shout to Him to fill you...and He will when you meet Him in the chambers!

Chapter V

Deep Is Calling unto Deep

The word "deep" is defined as "extending far down from the top or surface." (Dictionary.com). That means the farther down you go from the top, the more definitive the word "deep" becomes.

The book of Ezekiel 47:1-12 says,

> *Then he brought me back to the door of the temple; and there was water, flowing from under the threshold of the temple toward the east, for the front of the temple faced east; the water was flowing from under the right side of the temple, south of the altar. He brought me out by way of the north gate, and led me around on the outside to the outer gateway that faces east; and there was water, running out on the right side.*
>
> *And when the man went out to the east with the line in his hand, he measured one thousand cubits, and he brought me through the waters; the water came up to my ankles. Again, he measured one thousand and brought me*

through the waters; the water came up to my knees. Again, he measured one thousand and brought me through; the water came up to my waist. Again, he measured one thousand, and it was a river that I could not cross; for the water was too deep, water in which one must swim, a river that could not be crossed. He said to me, "Son of man, have you seen this?" Then he brought me and returned me to the bank of the river.

When I returned, there, along the bank of the river, were very many trees on one side and the other. ⁸ Then he said to me: "This water flows toward the eastern region, goes down into the valley, and enters the sea. When it reaches the sea, its waters are healed. And it shall be that every living thing that moves, wherever the rivers go, will live. There will be a very great multitude of fish, because these waters go there; for they will be healed, and everything will live wherever the river goes. ¹⁰ It shall be that fishermen will stand by it from En Gedi to En Eglaim; they will be places for spreading their nets. Their fish will be of the same kinds as the fish of the Great Sea, exceedingly many. But its swamps and marshes will not be healed; they will be given over to salt. ¹² Along the bank of the river, on this side and that, will grow all kinds of trees used for food; their leaves will not wither, and their fruit will not fail. They will bear fruit every month, because their water flows from the sanctuary. Their fruit will be for food, and their leaves for medicine."

From the definition of the word "deep," my question to you is how much of God are you experiencing?

Within the vision of this chapter in Ezekiel, I see that we can be at four different levels in our walk with God—four varying depths of relationship with God. These differing depths are our choice, not God's. We decide how far we are willing to go with our LORD.

The first one that is stated in this chapter of Ezekiel:

Step In: Ankle Deep: You visit God once or twice a week to say hello. You like to listen to the worship, but you never enter in. You like the "cooling" feel to be here, but you don't allow yourself to become a part. You don't feel like getting wet; maybe you don't even want to be in the presence of God—many excuses in the mind of one. There is no positive paradigm shift; you think that you're just fine on the shore. Your feet might not be burning anymore, but the rest of yourself is still getting burned. Temporary relief does not bring eternal results. God doesn't just want to be your aspirin. He wants you to go deeper with Him so that you can experience His fullness! You can't do that standing on the shore ankle deep.

Knee Deep: You go little deeper; now your desire of being in the presence of God is getting better. You actually want to pray with words from your mouth. But the desire is immediately crushed by the idea of being late for work or an appointment. Therefore, you rush to get out as quickly as possible. You are still on the fence and too close to the shore. That means you will be active today, but tomorrow you will go back to the shore.

Waist Deep: This is the level where things start to get uncomfortable. You come to the crossroad where commitment intersects passion. In the book of Revelation 3:16, the Bible says, "So then, because you are lukewarm, and neither cold nor hot,[a] I will vomit you out of My mouth." This is the level many Christians find themselves. Our passion and desires of this world and the commitment to a deeper relationship with our LORD Jesus Christ have become a crossroad for us to decide which part to take. Going halfway with God will lead you to backslide; there is no middle ground!

Drowning: Swimmers: This is where you are so deep with God that your feet can't touch the ground. It is where faith and works intersect. In other words, you have faith in what God has done, is doing, and is about to do, but now you have to "work" at swimming. Swimmers move past how they feel and worship anyway. Swimmers move past how they look to others and take a stand for righteousness. Swimmers move past what they want and fulfill God's commands to reach everyone everywhere with the message of Christ. Being in the chambers with God makes you a great swimmer! When you go deeper with God, everything that you are sick from will be healed, and whatever you touch shall prosper. In the secret, in the quiet place, when you call onto the LORD, HE will answer you and show you deeper things that your mind cannot imagine and your eyes have never seen.

In the depth of God are the hidden treasures and the revelation of God, which blow over your life, and the manifestation will be evident in the physical. After Moses encountered God, he asked to see God. In the experience of seeing God—"*keren*" in Hebrew, which means "rays of light"—the glory of the LORD was shining upon him, and Aaron and the assembly of Israel were afraid to look upon him. Deep communion with God yields unprecedented physical manifestation of the glory of God.

Chapter VI

I Know Him, Not I Know about Him

The fundamental difference between knowing about God and knowing God is about personal relationships. Because God is a person, you can know "about" Him, but you don't really "know" Him until you have a personal relationship with Him. For instance, I can know about the prime minister, but I wouldn't say that I know him. To know him, I have to meet him and get to interact with him. We have to reveal things to each other and be willing to share in each other's lives. The staggering promise of the Bible is that we can know our LORD in this way and that He *wants us* to know Him and share in His eternal life! So many people today believe that they know God, the Savior, the King of Kings, but unfortunately, they only know about God: the facts. Just about everyone can say that they know about God; they can give the facts about God and how HE has worked through the Bible. All these things are widely known facts. But can you tell me what God desires most from you today or where God would have you be? There tends to be a majority of people with facts of knowledge of God, a Sunday morning theology. Yet God desires for us all to have a relational knowledge of HIM. The book of 1 Samuel 15:22 says, "Has the

Lord *as great* delight in burnt offerings and sacrifices, As in obeying the voice of the Lord? Behold, to obey is better than sacrifice, *And* to heed than the fat of rams." Isaiah 1:11 says, "'To what purpose *is* the multitude of your sacrifices to Me?' Says the Lord. 'I have had enough of burnt offerings of rams and the fat of fed cattle. I do not delight in the blood of bulls, Or of lambs or goats.'" God did not want sacrifices and offerings made to HIM by HIS people; HE wanted their time. God desires for us to seek HIM and spend time with HIM, that we may truly come to know HIM.

Let us take a married couple for instance. When a man and woman meet for the first time, they only know the basic facts about one another. It is not until they have been together for a while that they really start to have relational knowledge of one another and melt together as one. The same holds true for us in our walk with God. If we truly desire to know God, as HE desires to know us, then we will spend time with HIM and incorporate HIM into every part of our lives. God desires so much to have a meaningful and deep relationship with us that HE even took the initiative to reach out to us. He knocks at our heart's door; He wants to come in to us and be a part of our lives. He took the initiative to tell us all about Himself.

A relationship with God is not built by attending church a couple times a week. Not until we start to live a life that is full of God every minute of every day will we truly know HIM. We can know HIM by always being ready to listen to HIM in prayer and through HIS Word in our chambers.

Religion Kills

Let's first look at how we receive our faith. The Bible gives us two ways that God gives faith to each person. The first is common to all mankind. The first measure is found in Romans 12:

> 3 *For I say, through the grace given to me, to everyone who is among you, not to think of himself more highly than he ought to think, but to think soberly, as God has dealt to each one a measure of faith.*
>
> *Every one means every person. There is not a person who has ever existed that was not measured a portion of faith. God instills within our hearts the power to believe in the gospel so that we can obtain salvation.*

The Bible also states that God has put eternity in our hearts in Ecclesiastes 3:11. How can the Bible state that God has dealt to each person a measure of faith and then state that the wicked do not have faith? I believe the answer can be clearly understood by seeking understanding through the rest of Scriptures. Jesus made a fascinating statement that aids in our understanding of this subject in Mark 4:23-25:

> *"If anyone has ears to hear, let him hear.' Then He said to them, 'Take heed what you hear. With the same measure you use, it will be measured to you; and to you who hear, more will be given. For whoever has, to him more will be given; but whoever does not have, even what he has will be taken away from him.'"*

Jesus reiterates this principle on at least four different occasions in His teachings. Each person was indeed given a measure of faith by God, but take heed how you hear, for if we reject the Word, God will take away what He has given. All faith is given by the mercy of God, and God has indeed extended His mercy on all; however, the Bible also states that God will not always strive with man. The wicked are those who reject the faith God has given as they resist the truth of God.

Consider this passage from Romans 1:17-19:

> *"For in it the righteousness of God is revealed from faith to faith; as it is written, 'The just shall live by faith.' For the wrath of God is revealed from heaven against all ungodliness and unrighteousness of men, who suppress the truth in unrighteousness, because what may be known of God is manifest in them, for God has shown it to them."*

Notice how this passage begins—God reveals Himself through faith. Only after God draws us by faith through our faith will He reveal His wrath against the unrighteous. God manifests Himself to each person, and then we either respond by faith or suppress the truth within our heart. God reveals the truth to all. God deals with some people over time as He draws them out of the misconceptions and misunderstanding and toward the truth of His gospel. I firmly believe that God knows each one's heart and deals with us until our spiritual eyes have been opened. Once God has shown Himself to them, then He holds each person accountable for the gospel. When the truth is suppressed, faith is lost. Don't miss the important truth that God does not turn someone over to a debased mind until after they suppress the truth. A person may indeed be corrupt and wallowing in the mire of their sins, but God does not reject us for our sins, but for our refusal of His righteousness. God tested Abraham; Abraham responded by immediate obedience. His obedience was the works that justified Abraham. It was not what Abraham did for God; it was his obedience out of faith that justified him and proved that his faith was alive. If Abraham believed that God *could* raise Isaac but then disobeyed God, that belief was meaningless and his faith would have been dead. If you believe God and obey, your faith is alive. If you live in apathy or rebellion, you have no faith regardless of what you claim to believe. Everyone claims to have faith, but the only faith that means anything is the faith that is quickened by the Spirit of God. Our faith is alive when we believe God and obey His commandments. When the Spirit stirs in our hearts, we must act in obedience by faith, or our faith is in vain.

Matthew 23:23-28 says,

> *Woe to you, scribes and Pharisees, hypocrites! For you pay tithe of mint and anise and cumin, and have neglected the weightier matters of the law: justice and mercy and faith. These you ought to have done, without leaving the others undone. Blind guides, who strain out a gnat and swallow a camel!*
>
> *Woe to you, scribes and Pharisees, hypocrites! For you cleanse the outside of the cup and dish, but inside they are full of extortion and self-indulgence. Blind Pharisee, first cleanse the inside of the cup and dish, that the outside of them may be clean also. Woe to you, scribes and Pharisees, hypocrites! For you are like whitewashed tombs which indeed appear beautiful outwardly, but inside are full of dead men's bones and all uncleanness. Even so you also outwardly appear righteous to men, but inside you are full of hypocrisy and lawlessness.*

There they were, only days after the triumphal entry into Jerusalem from Jesus and hours before the preparations for Passover began. All of the religious elite had come out to test and discredit Jesus in the eyes of the people, and they couldn't do it. Jesus had shut them down and silenced them with His response. Now Jesus publicly took the scribes and Pharisees to task, and the hypocrisy and false faith of the Pharisees was on full display before the people as the Son of God spoke the truth. Jesus then turned His attention to the scribes and Pharisees, starting a litany of woes (either seven or eight, depending on your Bible translation). In the first few woes, Jesus condemned the Pharisees as false teachers. They were obstacles against others entering the kingdom of heaven, and they themselves never entered either. They had deceived the defenseless and acted in destructive ways against them. They went out to convert Gentiles but converted them to greater condemnation, insulating them against the truth of the real knowledge of God. They were blind to God's holiness and taught people to devalue the righteousness of God. The Pharisees may have been the teachers of Israel, but they were terrible teachers, dangerous to everyone around them!

In the next three woes, Jesus looks at them a bit more personally. Earlier, He had looked at their teaching; now He looks at their character. He had already condemned their false teaching, and now He looks at their false faith. They had an appearance of holiness, but in reality, they knew nothing of the real righteousness of God. In fact, they did not know God at all, and Jesus exposes their dead faith for what it is.

In all of the harsh words from Jesus, please do not miss His compassion. False faith needs to be exposed. How else will someone be aware of the need? The Pharisees, like many today, were deceived about their relationship with God. They believed their outward appearance was proof of their holiness, when in reality, it was all hypocrisy. God does not want us to be deceived by false faith! He wants us to know what real life is in real faith as we walk with Him. Beloved, don't qualify effectiveness to dead religion by emphasizing more on your church attendance than your personal secret chamber time with God. God doesn't consider a hypocrite who teaches about ways to be more Christlike when they are not Christlike. A twelve-year-old boy was waiting for his first orthodontist appointment and was a bit nervous. Apparently, he wanted to impress the dentist. On the patient questionnaire, in the space marked "Hobbies," he had written, "Swimming and flossing" (*Reader's Digest* [8/94], p. 112).

That is a humorous example of how we are all prone to hypocrisy. But spiritual hypocrisy is not humorous; it is a dangerous and deadly sin. The hypocrisy of professing Christians has served as an excuse for many to disregard the claims of Christ, saying, "The church is full of hypocrites." The hypocrisy of Christian leaders has caused many believers to stumble. While Jesus was tender with many notorious sinners, He used scathing language to denounce those guilty of religious hypocrisy.

The story of Ananias and Sapphira warns us of the danger of the sin of hypocrisy. It was literally deadly for this couple. Someone has said that if God dealt with all hypocrites in the church as He dealt with this couple, our churches would become morgues! We are not told whether or not Ananias and Sapphira were true believers in Jesus Christ. Some argue that they were; some that they were not. Perhaps we are not told because if we knew that they were not true Christians, we would shrug their story off as not applying to us. If we knew that they were true Christians, we might say, "Thank God that this was just a one-time occurrence!" We would not pause and ask ourselves, "Is my faith in Christ genuine? Do I need to deal with the sin of hypocrisy?" We do know that Ananias and Sapphira were a part of the early church. Their story applies to us all! We need to be clear on the exact nature of the sin of Ananias and Sapphira. Their sin was *not* that they had sold their property and had given only a part to the church. In fact, Peter makes plain in Acts 5:4 that it would not have been a sin for them to have sold their property and not given anything to the church. Their sin was that they conspired together to deceive the apostles and the church into thinking that they were giving the entire amount, when in fact they kept back a portion for themselves. In other words, they were trying to impress everyone with a higher level of spirituality and commitment than they really had. Have you ever done that? I hope you do not say no, or we might need to have a sudden funeral today! We've all been guilty of trying to impress others with our commitment and devotion to Christ, even though we know in our heart that we are exaggerating. A pastor had been preaching on the importance of daily Bible reading. He and his wife were invited over to a parishioner's home for dinner. His wife saw a note on the kitchen calendar: "Pastor/Mrs. for dinner—Dust all Bibles" (*Reader's Digest* [3/90], p. 129).

Liberal commentators are shocked at this sudden, severe punishment. Ananias is not given a chance to repent, even though his sin seems not all that serious. His wife is not even told of her husband's death and of what will happen to her if she lies. The instant that she agrees with her husband's lie, she is struck dead. In this age of tolerance, we might think, *What's the big deal?*

But we need to view this sin from God's holy perspective, not from our world's relativistic view. Jesus always hit hypocrisy hard. He warned His disciples in Luke 12:1, saying, "Beware of the leaven of the Pharisees, which is hypocrisy." Like leaven, hypocrisy starts small and unnoticed. It doesn't seem to be a big deal. But if it is not quickly checked, it spreads. It deceives the person into thinking that things are right between him and God, when in reality, things are very wrong. This couple that fell into this sin were professing Christians, "members" of the church in Jerusalem. This means that we're all in danger of falling into this subtle sin. We don't want other Christians or those outside the church to think that we have problems. That wouldn't be a good testimony, would it? So, we put on our spiritual mask when we're around others, even though we know and our family knows that we do not live as we profess to live. When a prominent Christian is shown to be a hypocrite, the world heaves a sigh of relief, thinking, *Christians are really no different than anyone else. If they're phonies, then Christianity must not be true.*

One cannot claim daily secret chamber time with God when they are not actually doing it. Remember, the lack of or the inconsistency in our daily secret chamber time with God breeds the state of dead faith and hypocrisy.

Chapter VII

How Do I Do It?

Many usually would ask the question, Pastor, how do I get a consistent personal prayer or devotional life? I am glad you are thinking of the ways to get back to the divine intimacy with the LORD. I suggest starting your day by committing some time in prayer and in reading the Word of God. To beat the spirit of religion, it should not be time target met but rather daily consistency target. Such removes the burden and often tedious demand of fulfilling a religious duty, which eventually cause many to quit in a short period of time. Rather, target growth by being seriously consistent irrespective of the time spent. You should rise early enough so interruptions from other family members and phone calls don't break up your time with the Lord. The Bible says in the book of Mark 1:35, *"Now in the morning, having risen a long while before daylight, He went out and departed to a solitary place; and there He prayed."* This is the model of the life of Jesus, early in the morning, to go to a quiet place to talk to the Father. It is imperative to find that quiet moment or quiet place in the presence of God to talk to your LORD. Nobody was able to know what the high priest encountered when he went to the holy of holies to talk to God. This special moment in the presence of God makes you be able to speak to God genuinely about the life you are living in Christ and the rejuvenation of the Holy Spirit in your life. Furthermore, these serious consistent sessions increase as you go along daily in your personal prayer moments in the presence of God. Get devotional supports: first look, life group/sermon notes, inductive Bible study, "committed reading" through devotional guide. Obey a verse a day: Paul says Timothy has "carefully followed my doctrine, manner of life." (2 Timothy 3:10). That means he had the habit of living Scripture in his daily life.

These are the steps to enjoying the Chamber of the Holy of Holies:

1) Set aside time every day to have your devotionals. Try to keep it around the same time every day so it will be easier for you to develop this into a regular habit. If for any reason you are unable to complete your regularly scheduled devotional time, have a backup plan in place. It is important to be committed enough so that if you miss a day, you immediately pick up where you left off. Note that missing several days in a row for other pursuits is counterproductive to an effective devotional life.

2) Obtain materials you can use for spending time in the chambers. Outline chapters of the Bible you want to study. You can get daily devotional booklets from your church or online.

3) Choose a location or place for your secret chamber of devotion. It should be a quiet place where you can focus on the devotional

topic and reflect on its meaning to you personally. Most people choose a spot in their home away from other people, although a location outside can work too.
4) Focus continuous daily devotional time in the chambers.

Note that any effective devotional life must include a consistent habit and pattern of studying the Word of God and prayer. Why must my devotional life include Bible study? It is because Bible study for a believer is our foundation which is able to make us grow in our walk with God.

CONCLUSION

In this note, we must agree with the psalmist, who states the importance of the chamber in Psalms 84, which says:

> How lovely *is* Your tabernacle,
> O Lord of hosts!
> My soul longs, yes, even faints
> For the courts of the Lord;
> My heart and my flesh cry out for the living God.
> Even the sparrow has found a home,
> And the swallow a nest for herself,
> Where she may lay her young—
> *Even* Your altars, O Lord of hosts,

The Chamber of HOLY OF HOLIES

My King and my God.
Blessed *are* those who dwell in Your house;
They will still be praising You. Selah
Blessed *is* the man whose strength *is* in You,
Whose heart *is* set on pilgrimage.
As they pass through the Valley of Baca,
They make it a spring;
The rain also covers it with pools.
They go from strength to strength;
Each one appears before God in Zion.[b]
O Lord God of hosts, hear my prayer;
Give ear, O God of Jacob! Selah
O God, behold our shield,
And look upon the face of Your anointed.
For a day in Your courts *is* better than a thousand.
I would rather be a doorkeeper in the house of my God
than dwell in the tents of wickedness.
For the Lord God *is* a sun and shield;
The Lord will give grace and glory;
No good *thing* will He withhold
From those who walk uprightly.
O Lord of hosts,
Blessed *is* the man who trusts in You!
AMEN

About The Author

Prophet Kofi Ofori Yeboah is the founder and Senior Pastor of Life Renewal Charismatic Church (LRCC Ministries) in Montreal, Canada.

Supernaturally and with physical evidence, the Holy Spirit has transformed many lives through this dynamic ministry.

Flowing in prophetic, healing, and teaching anointings, he has proven to be an essential voice to the nations.

With over a decade of practical preaching, teaching, and counseling, Prophet Kofi effectively conveys the love of God toward others in understanding and love.

Prophet Kofi is currently spearheading a number of events such as the "Faith Nuggets Broadcast," the School of Ministry, and annual prayer revivals and leadership conferences in cities across the world. Kofi brings the pulpit to the pew, weekly applying God's wisdom and divine pragmatism to today's world solutions. His ministry goal is to make Christ's teachings, supernatural power, and churches relevant for today.

He has mentored many who are spearheading different aspects of ministry in the kingdom as well as in the business and governmental arenas across the world.

Kofi is a husband, father, conference speaker, counselor, and mentor. He and his wife, Henrietta Ofori Yeboah, are the proud parents of Janai, Zoey, and Raphael.

Follow Prophet Kofi on Instagram (@Pastor_kofiyeb) or follow him on Facebook (Kofi Yeboah) for a daily inspirational word and announcements of his next event dates.

For bookings, to register for the School of Ministry, or to host Prophet Kofi in your city for inter-city revivals, please send your email to: info@lrccministries.com or call 1-855-200-0602 EXT.204

Stay up to date with Prophet Kofi's latest sermons by downloading the "I Am LRCC" Ministry app on the Google Playstore and the Apple Store, and be part of the LRCC community!